You Can't Play the Game If You Don't Know The Rules

A Guide for Teens and Young Adults Transitioning into Adulthood

CHEYENNE D. BOYD

Copyright © 2015 Cheyenne D. Boyd

All rights reserved. No part of this book may be reproduced or transmitted in any form or by any means, electronic or mechanical, including photocopying, recording, or by any information storage and retrieval system, without permission in writing from the copyright owner.

ISBN-10: 0692498923
ISBN-13: 978-0692498927

Edited by Lea M. Brown

Cover photo by Mario D. Peterson

DEDICATION

To Young People who need just a little inspiration, guidance and direction. Go Get It.

Table of Contents

Intro 7

Lesson 1: To Play the Game, You Must Know the Rules 9

Lesson 2: Signing Up For the Team: What You Need To Know (Code of Conduct) 15

Lesson 3: Do, Go, HAVE: Life Rewards ACTION! 24

Lesson 4: Choices, Choices, Choices…& Consequences 27

Lesson 5: Now That You Know The Rules, How Will You Play The Game? 36

Lesson 6: Word Is Bond…Never Go Back On Your Word 42

Lesson 7: How To Ask For Things You Need the Right Way 47

Lesson 8: The Tale Of Two Extremes: Those Who Take It All, and Those Who Never Ask—Why Both Are Bad 55

Lesson 9: The Draft --- Choose Your Crew & Teammates Wisely 60

Lesson 10: Programs = Opportunities: Choose and Use Them Wisely 67

Outro: Game On!!! 72

INTRO

So what makes an athlete the best athlete? What makes an employee become the employee of the month? What makes a couple stay together for many years or a person who has maintained the same job for years? All these people understand that stumbling is a part of the journey. Griping over problems, things they don't have, and remaining angry about it does not propel one to success. They understand there is a process to getting ahead. You must study and work at the system and learn how to make it work for you.

Lesson 1:
To Play the Game, You Must Know the Rules

What does football, basketball, baseball, tennis, soccer, golf, even Monopoly, Solitaire, and Candy Crush, have in common? These games have rules!

Let's pretend you're a person who doesn't know much about football. All you know is you must take the ball, run down the field, and if you reach the end zone you score! Woo Hoo! Six points! Then you put the ball through the big H-shaped thing at the end, you get one more point! You know if you keep doing that over and over, whichever team ends with the most points wins!!! Yeah! Spike the ball! Do your happy dance in the end zone!

Learning about life is very much like learning a

game. You may have seen the game, you may have hung out with people who play the game, you may have even played the game, but the rules may have been for the game at that age and at that level. Now, as an adult, the game is at the greatest level and. You may not know all the rules because the rules aren't the same as pee wee football or tee ball. You're in the major leagues now! The rules are from the National Football League or Major Baseball League. When you make a bad play or act unreasonably, you will be fined, traded, or kicked off the team. It's all based on the choices you make and how you go about making them.

It's the same with life. All these years, you've been living your life. You have grown up watching people go about living their lives, going to the grocery store, going to school, watching folks cook and eat everyday. You know that people live in a house or apartment or something like that. You know people get their groceries at a store. You know people buy clothes. Then there are holidays, events and parties that come. People have jobs and cars and stuff. The difference is that you thought to have all of this was much easier than it turned out. And why it's not is

YOU CAN'T PLAY THE GAME IF YOU DON'T KNOW THE RULES

....because you don't know all the rules.

I'm here to tell you, you'll never know all the rules. As soon as you think you know them, they will change. To know the basics and to know where to go to find the rules is an essential part of life. See, the one thing that is constant in life is change. Change will always happen.

Ok, back to the game. You're playing football, and you're the running back. I throw you the ball. You catch it and begin to run towards the goal. BAM!!! Someone hits their helmet smack dab on the ball you're running with, and the ball pops out of your grasp. FUMBLE!!!! The other team grabs the ball and scores a touchdown. What are you doing when this is going on? You're yelling at the referee saying, "He just took my ball, tell him to give me my ball back! That is not fair!"

You already know what I'm going say: yup, life isn't fair (I thought you'd figure that out by now!) The reason you're rolling your neck at the referee is because you don't know all the rules to the game! See, it's not the world's job to do that for you. It's not the world's job to make sure you comprehend everything there is to know. Especially when you were under the age of 18, people would not let you make hardly any decisions about your life. But now as a legal adult, you are solely responsible for everything you say and do. Now when you sign on the dotted line, your signature is stating that you know what you're doing and responsible for anything that happens after that. Amazing huh?

As you learn the rules of the game, you become more mature, and you recognize what's a block, a hold, a fumble, etc. You later learn that if you rush the kicker or interfere with the receiver, you get a penalty. You can penalize the team and you can get fined by the league. You see, that's what happens when you don't follow the rules.

Same in life. When you learn more of the rules, you can make better decisions about your life. You can predict what will happen if you do this or don't do that. Some decisions are just common sense, but I'm learning that common sense is no longer common. That's why I'm writing this book.☺

Life Rules

When you emancipate, grow up, and leave to be on your own, there are adult rules you need to know: life rules. Life goes in a circle in all aspects, and when you get these rules down, life will be simpler and easier. What is the circle of life? It means there are seasons to everything. Every year, we know at the beginning there's a New Year, eventually a Memorial Day, a Fourth of July, a Labor Day, Thanksgiving and Christmas. Every year there are four seasons. Even though you cannot predict the future, you can give an educated guess about what will happen in the future based on what has happened in the past and what's done now. For example, the Friday after Thanksgiving is Black Friday, and many stores will have bargain prices for all types of gifts. You know this, and you prepare to purchase something you may not have the opportunity to purchase at any other time.

It's the same with everything else; shorts and T-shirts will come to the stores in the spring. Coats show up in the fall. You will need air conditioning in the summer and heat in the winter. Those things you must be aware of to prepare for when they come around.

You Must Learn the Rules

If you are in a place that has rules, follow them. There are two types of people in this world: people who follow the rules, and people who think they're the exception to the rule. If you think you're the exception, you're in for a world of hurt!

Rules are in place because of people like you! If everyone paid on time, arrived at their appointments on time, etc., life would be rosy. But nooo! People that think they are the exception to the rules come along always wanting a little more time, money or special favors. Listen, just follow the rules!

Lesson 2:
Signing Up For the Team: What You Need To Know (Code of Conduct)

When you were a young kid, what did you say when someone asked you what you wanted to be when you grew up? Did you say you wanted to be the president, a princess, a rock star, Michael Jackson, Wayne Gretzky, Peyton Manning, LeBron James? More than likely, people said, "Yessss, you can be whoever you want to be!" Great, right? But no one explained it takes a lot of work, commitment, planning, even positioning to become the next Michael Jackson or LeBron James. Some folks even ask great high school and college athletes who they want to be, and many say Michael Jordan or Tom Brady. At least those kids are playing the game, but some of you out there haven't even stepped up to the plate, never played a sport in your life! You have dreams and aspirations, but no preparation for how to get it. For some ridiculous, outlandish reason, you think someone is just supposed to give it to you. It's the same about life. You can't go to school when you feel like it, leave home, foster care, etc. and think you're moving into a condo with central air, an enclosed garage, and lawn service!

Before signing up for the "team" of adult life, here are some things you need to consider:

Things You Need to Do When Moving Out On Your Own

You need an A, B, C plan. Plan A is often your dream plan, what you want to do. If you want to go to the NBA or NFL, be a doctor, lawyer, writer, singer, dancer, etc. Plan A is your dream job/career/life path. Plan B is the plan you can afford, usually short term goals allowing for all the things to get you into the right places so you can complete the next steps. Plan C is if plan B doesn't work and so on. Usually plan "A" is out of your reach initially, plan "B" is doable, but money, people, places or time always get in the way of making it go smoothly. Plan "C" is what occurs when plan "A" and "B" doesn't work out exactly as planned but reminds you that you still must keep moving forward.

Have enough common sense to know what you have, what you don't have, and what must be done to get what you need.

Things you must consider:

- Where will l live?

- How much do I need to live there?

- How much do I need to eat?

- How will I get transportation?

Who will be able to help me when I need it? And who else? And who else? And who else? (This doesn't always mean financially, it means with advice, direction, resources).

When leaving the home and embarking on a new independent life, you'll need to obtain and keep the following things in a safe place if needed for future use: your birth certificate, social security card, immunization record, and an I.D. These are the basic things needed to receive housing, money, and a job.

Why a job you ask? Because money does not reproduce on its own, You need it to live! You need it to pay your rent, buy groceries, buy clothes, hygiene products, to continue to become the best you. Even when you stay with a friend, family, foster parent or former foster parent, it is not their expectation for you to freeload forever! (For many, not even a little while.) A person once told me that someone was staying in his home until they could get on their feet. He said the guest had to leave because no one is going to lay around his house when he leaves for work and still be in bed when he comes home - not while he pays the bills! My mother explained to me at a young age that no one lives in their home for free. Even if the house is paid off, there's still insurance, taxes and utilities to pay.

Even pet dogs bark to give warning that someone is coming. The dog has a job (responsibility) as well. Why would you think you don't?! Shucks, some folks won't even do that! If you can't contribute to the household, sometimes the best thing to do is leave. Why? Because you want to maintain the relationship, not end it. Sometimes, the only way peace can win is by living on your own.

The truth is your family, friends, parents and foster parents care about you but understand: people will no longer take care of you. You must care for yourself! To do that, you must recognize the way you go about making a life for yourself: it's not easy, but your decisions determine if your quality of life will be good or bad.

Independence: The Basics

Get a notebook/folder and some plastic sheet protectors that fit in the notebook/folder. Place your birth certificate, social security card, immunization records, school papers, financial aid paperwork, emancipation court papers, lease, medical card, or any other important paperwork inside. Always put it back in the notebook after it's needed. The plastic can help keep your papers from getting torn, wet, or lost. If you need anything important, someone will always ask for one or all of these things, and you not having them can make you wait so much longer than you want with the process.

Keep them in a safe place and only get them when needed. Carry identification daily, but do NOT carry your birth certificate or social security card with you daily. If you misplace your wallet or purse, unfortunately, people can use your social security number, and other information to steal your identity. Identity theft is when someone steals your sensitive information, especially your social security number, and they can make purchases in your name, as you. They don't plan on paying for anything, and you're the one who gets the bill. It sometimes takes years to get your credit straightened out again where companies trust you are who you say you are It could be difficult to open a credit card, buy a car, house, etc. Needless to say it's not a good situation, so keep your information private!

How to Find Housing

There are five options for housing:

YOU CAN'T PLAY THE GAME IF YOU DON'T KNOW THE RULES

1. Pay for it…rent, that is

2. Live with family or friends

3. Live in campus housing

4. Apply for subsidized or transitional housing

5. A Shelter (when all else fails, you can go to a shelter- just know they also have rules that you must abide by)

   http://www.homelessshelterdirectory.org

We'll focus on the first **four** options below:

1) Pay For It

When renting an apartment, most landlords will conduct background checks to see if you have any criminal history. They don't want any crimes being committed on their properties. (And I'm sure the other tenants would prefer it that way, too) They also want a security deposit and first month's rent. At the cheapest, you'll need approximately $1000.00 just to move in. This doesn't include utilities (gas, electric and water, etc.) Some utilities have deposits you must pay. At times, the price of rent can include utilities, but that doesn't happen often. But if it does, the lowest rent communities hover around $500/month.

2) Live With Family or Friends

Living with family or friends is great. It gives you an opportunity to save money to move out on your own, share rent and utilities with a roommate you trust, or to have a place to stay while you focus on school.

Know that it's a gift to live in a family member's home while working part-time. Always prepare for your next step, as this is not permanent. The same respect must be given to friends who live together. One's decision can impact how the other can live. Do your best to respect each other's privacy and living space.

3) Live In Campus Housing

I'm talking about a dorm or campus apartment that may be a part of your college room and board. Seek out grants, work-study, scholarships, and loans (Remember loans must be re-paid) that can be obtained to live reasonably while in school.

Remember: during the winter, spring and summer breaks, you need a place to go. Plan early and wisely!

4) Apply for Subsidized or Transitional Housing

Apply for subsidized housing as soon as you're able! Why? Because it can take years to obtain. For subsidized housing, it may take years to get into, and you might not know what your situation will be like two years from now. Transitional housing is great for those who can get in. It provides a stable-yet-temporary housing situation that gives you time to gain income, furniture, household items and other things before receiving the expense of being independent all at once.

LESSON 3:
DO, GO, HAVE: LIFE REWARDS ACTION!

Some people have the ridiculous idea that opportunity will magically knock on their door one day, instead of them going to get it. Please understand that **Life Rewards Action!** You can't sit around waiting for things to happen for you. If you lay around and dream about it, but don't do what you said you were going to do, then nothing is going to happen! You have to GO GET IT. Do what you need to make a life for yourself (provided it's legal).

For instance, if you don't produce income to keep your lights and heat on, they'll get turned off. If you don't go to work to pay your rent, you'll get evicted. If you don't kick out those people doing drugs in your

YOU CAN'T PLAY THE GAME IF YOU DON'T KNOW THE RULES

place, you're allowing people to take advantage because **you** didn't do anything about it, which can lead to **you** getting evicted! It's because **you** refused to do it! Life rewards those who take action! With that said, **you** must know what to do. First you must know what you want, need, and then plan how to get it.

It makes me cringe when I speak to young people and they say, "I'm going to get a job!" Do you understand that you are already way behind in the planning process? Before you go out on your own, you should already have a job, you should have money saved. You should have plates, silverware, a place, and have the job that gives you the means to pay for it. If you don't, then you should at least have the ability to find the job, and the resources to help you. Also, have the attitude that any opportunity and assistance that comes your way is a blessing that's been bestowed on you to help you move to the next phase in your life.

Open your mind to every opportunity that comes your way. If you act on it, it may surprise you where it could lead!

A young lady came into the office saying that she was homeless. After staying at her friend's house for three months, her friend threw her out. After gathering information and recognizing what she had been through, it was obvious she desperately needed help. However, she missed her appointments, and failed to follow through on her obligations. She was now rushing others to get her a place to live. Should everyone stop everything they have going on to place her priorities first, when she didn't make her own priorities first? She did little, so she gets little.

Life rewards action, family!!! Now get to moving!!!!

LESSON 4:
CHOICES, CHOICES, CHOICES…& CONSEQUENCES

In Lesson 3, I talked about how life rewards action. Now you must understand how your actions and the choices you make have consequences. Let's work at making better choices to have the best outcomes. See, a consequence can be getting paid at the end of the week after going to work every day, or begging for money so you can eat after not finding a job.

Let's say you choose to have sex between 16 to 25 years of age. That choice can affect you for the rest of your life. What if you get pregnant? You can choose to have an abortion **or** you can choose to carry the baby to term and put it up for adoption, **or** you can choose to raise the baby. But no matter what your choice is, that decision will affect the rest of your life. Let's say you choose to have the child and raise it as a single-parent. Now you have to choose how you'll provide for the baby, how you'll care for the baby, where you live, and how you'll pay your bills. The child is totally dependent on you. Your thoughts and dreams of attending school, finding employment, etc. are now even more important because it affects your child, too. Then, there are more choices, challenges, and decisions! It never ends. Life is one big choose fest! Be sure you make the best choices that not only affect you now, also think about how that choice will affect you long term, years from now.

Bad Decisions

If you make a bad decision, don't continue to make it worse with even more bad decisions! You know what I'm talking about; when the utility cuts off your power, don't call and argue with the representative. Now when you finally pay it so it can get reconnected, they may not send someone out as fast as you would like. If you get in a fight and the police are called, let's not continue to fight in front of the police. I can hear you now, "I don't care what the officer says it's me and you at 3 o'clock!" O.o You are going to jail!

I get it! Sometimes decisions are made out of an emotional state of mind. Someone made you angry, sad, etc., but you still must think about the ramifications of your actions. Sometimes people don't realize little things that can make a bad decision even worse. For instance, Allen was stopped by the police for speeding. Allen thought it would be smart to tell them his name was Patrick. Once the police found out, not only did Allen get a ticket for speeding, but he also got a charge of misrepresentation of identity and alluding arrest. Allen just made a bad problem worse. He could have simply paid the ticket, and it would be over. Now, he still has to pay the ticket, but also show up in court for two more charges. Allen made a bad decision way worse.

I'll give another example. This is something that

doesn't happen often, but when it does, it's in the news:

Let's say a 16 or 17-year-old girl has sex (quite possibly the first decision that was made that wasn't a good one). Another bad decision was her and her partner didn't use protection. A few weeks later she finds out she's pregnant. OMG! What does she do now? She thinks her parents will kill her, so she goes on like it isn't happening. She has life plans, she was promised a car or job, and the baby wasn't in the equation. So she doesn't tell her parents that she's pregnant. Well, doing nothing doesn't help. Fast forward nine months later and she's delivering a baby in the bathroom stall at school, or she may leave the baby in an alley or on the doorstep of a church. This is an example of a person making a choice to have unprotected sex that leads to them getting pregnant and abandoning a baby. An innocent child abandoned, just based on one initial decision to have unprotected sex! Was the initial decision the greatest? Maybe not, but then the decisions made after that made a bad situation even worse. You may say, look, lady, this is an extreme example. But actually, this happens more than you may think! This is the reason we have safe-haven laws. (Safe-haven laws protect parents who leave their new babies up to 30 days old in a hospital or emergency center without any abuse or harm from being prosecuted.)

If you're aware you made one bad decision, try to make it better, not worse! The teenage girl was aware of her bad decision leading to her pregnancy. She probably should have told her parents, but since she was afraid to do so, the next thing she probably should have done was sought help from another adult source (Planned Parenthood, a guidance counselor at school, a mentor, a pastor, etc.). A trusted person or organization would have been able to give insight to her situation.

Use wisdom regarding the decisions you make. Before you make a decision, take a minute to think about the consequences of each choice. Look into the future and see the consequences of your choices as if they were happening now, in the present.

When we have many choices in life, it can be difficult to decide what's the best choice. If you want to learn how to make better decisions in life, consider these steps:

Ms. Chey's 6 Steps to Decision Making:

1). Identify the severity of the situation/decision

Is it a simple decision between chips or popcorn, or is it something life changing like to rent a house or buy a car? The more important the decision is, the more time you may have to spend thinking about it before choosing.

2). Gather information for each choice, or ask for advice

In case of the chips or popcorn, what brand, how old, which has the best flavor? In renting a house or car, what can I afford, how much is the insurance or utilities, can I save, etc.?

What are the consequences (good or bad) of your choice? List them!

Examples:

- Popcorn in the teeth may cause me to go to the dentist.
- Chips are more fattening.

- But the popcorn is healthier.

In regards to a home:

- Is there enough room?
- Can I afford to live there?
- Is it easy to maintain?
- Is it close to the bus stop, department stores, grocery stores, etc.?

3). Determine what's important to you

Popcorn is great, but will get stuck in my teeth. Chips may be the best option for me. If I have no one to live with, then renting a one bedroom apartment may be the best thing for me.

4). Create your plan and take action to implement it

You choose the popcorn (you've decided it's healthier, and you can brush and floss afterward.)

You decide to rent a house. (Calculate the budget,

figure out the utilities and move in.) You get the idea.

In conclusion, figure out your situation, gather information, list the consequences, figure out what's most important, and then move toward implementing your best plan.

Also know if you choose to do nothing, stuff still happens....only it happens to you instead of for you! Life is going to happen! If you sit around avoiding things, stuff will still happen to you! Things happen every day: car accidents, bills are due, children are born, disease happens, and so does death. Even in that aspect you have choices: you can do nothing and wait for whatever happens, or you can do something.

Want to know what I mean, right? DeCarlo, an 18-year-old young man, planned on moving into an apartment. He saved money for the security deposit and first month's rent, but he forgot about the utilities (electric, gas and water) which include a deposit as well. Since DeCarlo didn't think about utility bills, he didn't pay the first month's bill, even though he had them turned on. Well, nothing happened. The utilities stayed on, but DeCarlo did not pay the second month's bill either. The lights, gas, and water stayed on one more month. On the third month when

DeCarlo got the bill, it included a shut-off notice; if the bill weren't paid by a certain date, the utility would get completely turned off. By DeCarlo not doing anything, stuff still happened to him. His bill grew and grew. Late fees were added to his balance, and now he's at risk of having no electric or gas. Without gas, there is no hot water and no heat in the winter. Without electric, you can't watch television or keep your groceries cold so your food will go bad. All because you chose not to do anything at all!

Make the best choices to benefit your life. If you realize you didn't make the best choice, learn from the experience and move forward based on the FAITH that GOD will work it out.

Lesson 5:
Now That You Know The Rules, How Will You Play The Game?

When You Know Better, You Do Better
~ Maya Angelou

When you learn the rules, the game (life) is great. Now you must implement the rules effectively. The object is simple: whoever makes the most points wins. But that's not all! You must know who you are playing with and against; the expectations for the team. You must practice, come up with a strategy, stay consistent, and play the best you can to win the game.

Here's an example, if you walk into Hooters wearing booty shorts and a halter top, then you might get the job, but McDonald's, not so much. Getting off the bus in pajamas pants on your way home, you assume no one sees you on the street. Later, you enter a nearby store and ask for an application. What you didn't realize is the manager at the store saw you walking down the street days earlier. You didn't see him, but he saw you wearing those same pajamas pants. Will you get that job? I think not! The first impression has already given the manager an idea of how you will present yourself to his patrons because that is the way you present yourself to the world. Is that the best you are giving? Always give your best self!

Then, there are times when you dress casually with a nice shirt and slacks. Your hair is neat, and you speak with respect. He may see you getting off the bus with your backpack that looked as if it was full of books. He notices you pick up an item from the ground and put it back. See, every time you present yourself to the world, you dictate the reactions others may have of you. The reactions may be positive or negative, but most times, you create how people see you. I'm not saying you shouldn't be yourself, not at all! What I am saying is that you must handle the reaction that comes with your choice. If you have red or blue hair and want a job as a receptionist at my law firm, your look doesn't fit my industry. It gives me the impression that your look might work best in an art gallery or a more casual industry. Don't expect others to think differently because you are different. Remember this.

Take for instance, tattoos. Body art is very common these days. I know people who have multiple tats, but you would never know because they are placed in strategic places. Strategic you say? Yes! Lisa owns a business, and even though she loves to express herself with body art, she also recognizes others may not share her views. Should people care? Maybe or maybe not. But as a business owner, Lisa wants people to focus on her business. On the other hand, John is eighteen years old and decided to express himself by placing a beautifully-illustrated tattoo of four skulls on his right cheek. He's a mild-mannered young man, but no one would know because his tattoo scares the living bejeezus out of people! When he began looking for jobs, it was harder than ever. Fast food companies wouldn't hire him because they said he would scare the kids and families that come in. He couldn't even get an interview for any customer service position, and the only possibilities he had were positions working away from the public eye.

What you must realize is that when you have a job, you're representing the company, what they stand for, and what they present to their customer/clients; in other words, you represent their brand and image. It could mean the difference between making money and not making money! For the company and for you!

John eventually obtained some factory jobs and landscaping work, and he found someone who connected him with a program that specializes in laser tattoo removal. It took years and many sessions to take the tattoo off of his face. If the program were not available, it would have cost him over $3000 to remove his tattoo!

As the subtitle of this lesson says, when you know better, you do better. Which leads me to my next point: Don't procrastinate!

If you have a problem, seek resources early instead of waiting until it is too late. Just because the electric didn't get cut off in July when you didn't pay the electric bill (nor August when you didn't pay it again), it doesn't mean they forgot about you! Now you think they're out to get you when they cut it off. Now you're stocking your fridge and stressed out because you must gather twice the amount of money to pay the entire bill, the reconnect fees and the late fees. Now you must find the money to replace the spoiled food in your fridge. All could have been avoided if you paid your bill or asked for help when the problem arose. Companies give assistance if they see consistency and effort. Call those places to see if there is assistance. Even if they don't offer assistance, they may know who does. Don't get mad at them, they're just following the rules! (The Home Energy Assistance Program, or HEAP, is a program that helps with energy utility assistance. Apply at your local utility assistance provider.)

Dirty Players

There are dirty players in the game. These are the cheaters, haters, trash talkers and smooth operators. It's the guy in the basketball game who always give the flagrant fouls. In hockey, it's the guy who hits you in

YOU CAN'T PLAY THE GAME IF YOU DON'T KNOW THE RULES

the head with the stick when the referee's not looking. In baseball, it's the one who puts tar on the bat or liquid on the ball.

There will always be people who try to take advantage of you, there will always be opposition. Some people lie and try to get the upper hand. It's your responsibility to know the rules when dealing with them. For instance, if you purchase a car, understand the difference between an "as is" and a warranty purchase. If it's from a dealership and a warranty is offered, what does that mean? It could mean the difference between paying nothing extra or thousands of dollars. Sometimes, because of not understanding the paperwork, you end up paying more. Oprah says, "If you have doubts, then don't." Ask someone you know to review any contract or dealings before you agree to anything.

LESSON 6:
WORD IS BOND: NEVER GO BACK ON YOUR WORD

If you have nothing else, you have your word! Your word is a very powerful thing. Use it wisely.

Has someone ever told you they were going to do one thing, then didn't do it? How did that make you feel? You probably thought they were a liar and can't be trusted. Sometimes there are so many people like that in your life, you feel you can't trust anyone, even professionals at times. But what you have is the **word you give.** I can't stress how important it is to do what you say you're going to do. If you can't do something, call and say you can't do it. Do not make any promises you can't keep.

First thing's first: Don't lie! People are less likely to trust you, even if caught in a lie once. Often, people tell lies and think they are getting away with it. What you don't know is two things are happening: 1) We know you are lying but realize you're in such a desperate situation, so instead of arguing with you in an attempt to get you to tell me the truth, we just help you in your dire situation, and 2) We realize you're simply trying to manipulate, and you're wasting our time. Kick rocks. People who offer assistance can tell the difference between those who really need help, and those who're asking to gain a service or resource only they don't come out of their own pockets to get what they WANT, not what they NEED.

For example, paying your bills on time is much like keeping your word. It shows you can be trusted and are a responsible adult. Rent and utilities are essential for your housing. Credit cards and car payments are essential for good credit. What you do with your money and how you prioritize your spending is the key to obtaining the upper hand in life. If your bills are not paid on time, you will eventually see a negative response (lights turned off, eviction, etc.) because you're not following the rules. Companies communicate with each other when you don't keep your word. The next time you go, they may turn you down for housing, credit cards, etc. because you now have a reputation of not being trusted to pay your bills on time. This keeps you from obtaining housing in the future, gets you denied for loans, etc. The results aren't good at all!

Making an appointment is like making a promise. Whether it's making an appointment to meet up with a friend, a doctor's appointment, or a meeting to discuss housing, you're promising to be there at a certain place at a certain time. Please be mindful that they are carving out time to spend just for you. If you come late or not at all, it's telling someone that 1) you don't respect their time, 2) you really don't want the information or resource that they are supplying, regardless if you need it or not.

It's a major pain when you cancel appointments without notifying the person/company you set up the appointment with. It's rude and extremely inconsiderate. If you make an appointment, keep it, and if you can't, let them know! Call as soon as you know you can't make it, it's simple, common courtesy. They are waiting for you, and if you couldn't make it, someone else could have your time slot. If people are taking the time to meet with you, be considerate enough to tell them you can't make it.

If you are unsure if you can commit to your appointments, ask if you can get back with them, check to see if it's possible, or give yourself time to complete the request. If you have nothing else to give, give your word and stick to it. There is nothing that a person will respect more than doing what you said you can or cannot do.

In essence, what this boils down to is keeping your promises. Don't make promises if you are unsure you can keep them. Don't tell a potential employer (or anyone for that matter) you can get there if you are not sure you can get there. Someone says, "You have the job, can you start tomorrow?" You have no idea when you can get there, no money to get the uniform, shoes, and supplies needed for the job do not say, "yes!" Who does that?! You are setting yourself up for failure. Instead, say, "May I call you back with the day I can start? Maybe in a week or two?" Even if you have family or friends who may help, giving them no time to help you can sabotage a job opportunity that can lead to an encouraging future. Plan, plan, plan.

Lesson 7:
How To Ask For Things You Need The Right Way

"God gave you two ears and one mouth because you're supposed to listen twice as much as you speak!"— G-Momma, Granny, Nana, Aunt Bea, Aunt Bobbie and 'em.

I've heard this all my life from my loved ones, and it's so true: half of all effective communication comes simply by listening.

Communication is used to effectively express your thoughts, feelings, needs, and desires. The key word here is effectively. Have you ever been in a setting when the people were speaking, and even though they were speaking in English, you are still left wondering what was said or what they meant? Well, that's based on what register of language they're using.

There are five major types of registers of language that are used in the English language every day:

1) **The Frozen Register** is that used when quoting the bible, or stating the pledge of allegiance. It's a standard monotone voice that all who says it sounds the same way.

2) **The Formal Register** is language used in presentations, speeches, etc. This register is one-way communication, sometimes a technical and defined interpretation of facts or information.

3) **The Consultative Register** is the third register that is between two parties. It is often seen between teacher/student or doctor and patient. It's often spoken with one in agreement with "yeses" and "um hmms." Interruptions are allowed and acceptable.

4) **The Casual Register** is often used among friends. The conversation most like two friends hanging out. Slang is used and interruptions happen all the time.

5) **The Intimate Register** is used with family and close relationships. It depends more on the intonation

of language used and vocabulary used with your family, siblings, spouses, boyfriend and girlfriends, or close family.

I explained the different registers because no matter where you're from or what language you speak, everyone uses them in everyday language at some point. The problem is, some people speak in the incorrect tone for the situation at hand. For instance, you may speak to others in an intimate or casual register when it should have been a consultative tone. If you use the intimate register when you speak with family, then speak to your doctor that way, he or she can get the wrong impression of you. Your words were communicated incorrectly, and you could potentially get the wrong information about your health, and your life. You'd never know what you are supposed to do next.

So, with that said, I would like you to learn how to use the correct registers for the correct situations. For instance, do not call a business or organization and start asking questions without a salutation. Always stay respectful and say "hello," maybe even state your name. Ask a direct question. Do not, and I repeat do not begin telling the person a story about what is wrong in your life. They'll end up responding with what they think you are requesting, which could be wrong and make you frustrated. Simply asking a direct question in a respectful manner will eliminate any frustrations and communication gaps. Let's say you're calling the doctor's office. You stubbed your big toe, so that's exactly what you should say at first. You shouldn't go into a story about how your uncle told you to go to the store and when you got back, you tripped up your steps inside your apartment because your hands were full of grocery bags when you returned from grocery store. The person receiving the information wants to know the direct problem, and then they will ask questions accordingly. Eventually, they'll ask questions in the "4 W's and How," the same things you learned in fourth grade: **what** happened, **when** it happen, **where** did it happen, **why** did it happen and **how**. At the current time, folks only want the facts. Giving them a story is time-consuming and does not get the results you want. If they need more info about the story, they will ask you to elaborate.

Let me explain: Celeste came to the office to ask for help in paying a utility bill. Instead of stating how much she needs, Celeste tells me how she ran out of gas, so she had to call a cab that made her pick up the kids late. The cab money used up her bill money, and that is why her electricity is off in her apartment. Celeste eventually gets to the point. The utility money was used to pay for the cab ride. Celeste is requesting help to pay her utility but took two hours to let someone know. Some people may ask why you didn't have the money, but be direct. Tell them the facts. They will ask the questions they need to have answered.

When you're making a request for a service or information, realize you're the one who needs help. You will always get more help by being nice rather than angry any day of the week. Always address people with "yes or no Ms., Mrs. or Mr." when addressing business people. Know your information. People are not there to guess what you want or what's wrong with you. Make sure you write information down if it relates to your business. When handling your business, have information like your account numbers, identification, birth certificates and social security cards, paperwork that relates to the situation. When you did what, where and how. Did you see those "W" questions come back?

Ok now. One little hack to make life easier is to write things down. You think "I'll remember that," but soon as you figure it out, it may change. The only thing constant in life *is* change! Listen, change is hard (for everyone!) It may take a while to get used to it, and when you finally understand it, it will change. Get something that works for you; a wall calendar, a notebook, the note application in your phone. Put information in that spot, so you remember what someone told you. If it's too much information that you didn't write it down, get the number to call and ask them again. Always, always, always write down the name of the person you are speaking with. If you have a problem later, the first thing someone will ask is, "Who did you speak with?" By knowing the name of the previous person you spoke with will make it easier for everyone involved. Secondly, write down what was said, what they are going to do, or who will do it. Let's say, Sherida came to get assistance from the Home Energy Assistance Program (HEAP). HEAP helps low-income residents with assistance on their gas or electric bills. Sherida's hours were cut back on her job in December. Living in Ohio, the weather gets very cold, and her gas bill can get up to $300 a month.

YOU CAN'T PLAY THE GAME IF YOU DON'T KNOW THE RULES

She was told she would pay only $25 per month on each utility for future months. To get the discounted rate, all she had to do was bring her identification, utility bills, social security card and last four pay stubs with her to the office. Sherida was so happy about only having to pay $25 per month, she forgot to write down that the worker asked for her to bring in her identification, and forgot to bring her ID. The worker told Sherida that she is unable to complete the application until she receives her identification. A few weeks went by, and Sherida received a shut-off notice from her utility companies. Now enraged, Sherida calls them wondering what happened. The utility explained that she only paid a partial payment on her bill. Sherida argues that she went to HEAP and was told she only needed to pay $25 on her bill. The utility explains that there is nothing on their system saying that she is on HEAP. An upset Sherida goes to the HEAP office to complain, only to remember she never returned with her ID. Sherida did not understand that without all proper paperwork, the application could not get processed. Sherida assumed that she did everything she needed to do, but she didn't realize how important it was to ask questions, write down the things required of her, and know that without her own follow through, her application would not be complete.

Follow up and follow through is necessary. No one is going to take care of you like you. Waiting on someone to call you back about your problem may take longer than you realize. Keeping track of your information and things that are important will always help you in business dealings later in life.

Lesson 8:

The Tale Of Two Extremes: Those Who Take It All, and Those Who Never Ask— Why Both Are Bad

There are people who will come to events only if there is a free giveaway, then take as much as they can. Their thoughts are not about anyone else, just what they can get for themselves. I'm not talking about taking an extra wrist band, or 2 or 3 water bottles; I'm talking about the whole dang box! These people are the ones who always have to have excess. They never get what they need but they get what they want regardless if they even need it. Be wary of them.

Then you have people who never ask for anything. The people who think they could do everything on their own. They feel that they can get the job, get the money, get the finances, get the transportation on their own and never ask anyone for help. They are an island unto their own selves. These people don't realize that it takes more than one person to create a relationship with others. These people don't recognize that you come into this world with help and you leave with help, but it's up to you to create relationships in between. Read these two stories about two young people named Mario and Armani to see what I mean:

Mario's Story:

Mario is a 19-year-old man and newly independent person who received the opportunity to move into his very first apartment. Unfortunately, Mario did not have any household items nor the money to buy any, so he found a place that donated household goods. Some of the items were used, and others were new. It included paper towels, toilet paper, dishes, brooms and mops, trash cans, etc. Another person assisted the young man with a truck to help transport the goods. When others took a second look at Mario's items, they found casserole dishes, Bundt cake pans, coffee makers and fifteen water glasses. Were these things awful to have? Not at all. But four months later when I visited Mario, I learned he needed a whole new set of dishes and silverware! He was also out of cleaning supplies and paper goods. When I asked what happened to his dishes, Mario stated that friends came over, ate on his dishes and would take his plates, silverware and glasses with them. I also found out later that Mario was not the greatest at washing his dishes, and after days of sitting in the sink, he'd just throw them away! Mario had no respect for the things he received and took for granted the opportunity he had.

Armani's Story:

Armani signed up for public housing but is still waiting. She was forced to move into a small apartment that was much more than she could afford. She moved there because it was the only place that she could take her dog. She didn't have friends who owned a truck to obtain donated items, nor did she have transportation getting here or there. She knew no one she could count on, but she was very independent and thought that she could do it all herself. Armani was given the opportunity for housing, but would not take it because the dog could not go, even though the apartment was free. She could have received so much assistance (food, household supplies, toiletries, etc.), but she would have rather did it on her own. Months later, I tried to call Armani, but her phone was disconnected.

So what did you learn from these two situations? Mario abused his opportunity, and Armani never seized hers; they both took their opportunities for granted. Mario just took, took and took. If he had other problems, his provider could say that he is at the limit of receiving. At least he gained some assistance and learned some tough lessons along the way. However, Armani will never get to learn hers, and she's now homeless once again.

These extremes are both bad because there is no balance. Find the balance: take advantage of some assistance, and be grateful for what assistance you DO get. Understand that making relationships with others and taking advantage of some assistance can be very helpful.

Lesson 9:
The Draft --- Choose Your Teammates Wisely

Have you drafted the right people in your life to benefit you? Do you want to chill with people who aren't going anywhere? Of course not! Or do you want to follow people going to college, getting jobs, having a household and car, people willing to create, do and learn things? Of course you do! Are you going to trust the person who stole a car last week? Who are you going to trust? Who will truly have your back?

Does your coach have a clipboard telling the team which way to move, where to go? Do you know what position you need to be in to defend your goal? Have you watched the game film over and over so you know the moves the player you are covering in the game will do? What if I told you that by the end of the season, you can be in the Finals? It all depends on your coaches, your teammates, and your opponents.

Finding a Coach

At times in your life, you'll need direction and guidance, a "coach" if you will. That person could be your parent, grandparent, aunts or uncles. It can also be a teacher, a mentor, a preacher, counselor or social worker. Usually someone older in your life who has life experience under their belt and who has your best interest at heart. They can advise you on the best choice to make.

Who's your favorite coach in this "game" of life? An Afrocentric modality states: if you arrive at the level where you want to develop into someone better, the best thing to do is become the student of someone more advanced in the path you want to follow.

You're probably asking yourself, "I've made up my mind about what I'm going to do, so why ask for help?" Once folks hear the advice guidance, the advice isn't as easy as they'd like it to be, so they choose to ignore the advice and go a completely different direction.

A coach or mentor is an experienced and trusted adviser, someone whom you admire and want to gain knowledge from to better your life. Mentors can sometimes be in your life for many years, so it's important to seek out a person you feel comfortable around and can trust.

Before you seek advice, you need to first ask yourself what path in life you want to follow. What are your dreams and goals? Ask the person if he or she can help you develop into someone better. Look at them as the expert, and you the student. Are they a good fit for where you're trying to go in life?

Think of it like this: between a car mechanic and LeBron James, who would you ask to change your oil, and who would you ask how to execute a layup? Would you ask the car mechanic how to play basketball? Of course not! But I'm sure you would want to ask LeBron first. I surely would! Don't get me wrong, the car mechanic may know a lot about basketball, but he or she isn't a master at it, and I surely don't want LeBron James working on my car! He may have some knowledge in caring for the mechanics of a car, but the mechanic has the direct knowledge in his specialized field.

Secondly, you must ask what's in it for them, and what's in it for me. When someone cares if you do well in life, the sheer satisfaction that you are well, successful, and developing your best self should be enough for them. If someone is looking to profit from your situation, then they aren't looking out for you. I've seen more friendships lost because of the "what can you do for me?" mentality. Sometimes, if you do what's advised (and meet the expectations) of a mentor who means well and want to see you succeed, then you should end up in a great place. It's simple: do what you're asked to do! And guess what? You still may not get the job, the apartment, the internship, the position, but that's life. Understand sometimes that you may fail. But as the cliché says, never give up! What's meant for you will be there just for you!

Finding Teammates

Guess what? You are the captain of your team.

Your "teammates" are your peers. They can be your best friends, classmates, coworkers, and are usually folks who like what you like and do what you do. Just like in sports, your teammates may be there for the rest of your life, or they may only be there for a season. But you are the one who gets to pick them. So who do you choose? You choose people you can trust, friends who will be there in good times and bad. You choose people who you give your time, who listen, give praise, and positive criticism; tell you when you're being dumb and telling you when you're brilliant. You choose people who encourage you and empower you. You choose people who tell you the truth, and who don't let you lie to yourself even when you maybe lying to everyone else. In life, a good "teammate" may not do what you do, but they may think how you think, value things you value, believe the same beliefs as you. Choose good people that have and show respect. Those type of teammates will never let you down and can assist you in winning the game of life!

Conquering Your Opponents

Then there are the opponents; you know the

ones: the "haters." They want what you have and (sometimes) purposefully get in your way. You know what I'm talking about! They're the managers at your job who criticize everything you do just to get on your nerves: the fries are too salty, your hat is crooked, or you forget to smile. Then there are the folks who try to take advantage of you. They know you don't know the rules and try to use you. And "opponents" are not just people, either. The "opponent" can be things or situations, challenges you must overcome. They can be classes and tests you must pass to graduate, bills you must pay. You just have to fight through these "opponents."

See, you must study your opponents, or the things that give you the most difficulty or problems. When you do, you'll know what your opponents will do, or what obstacles you will face, and you can bring better defense to your game.

Now that you've found trustworthy people who will keep their word, and don't have a selfish agenda, take your coaches, teammates, and your best "plays" to conquer your opponents. Your goal is to make the Finals and ultimately win the championship! For you, that could mean getting your dream job, dream home, dream family, dream car, or any life goal you want to achieve! Take every coach (mentor) and teammates (well-meaning friends) and use whatever you can to learn from your opponent's strategy to make it to the Finals (your ultimate life goals)!

Lesson 10:
Programs = Opportunities: Choose and Use Them Wisely

Let's say you're playing a video game. During your game, you've gone through all your lives and energy, and a commercial pops up saying you can gain another life or more energy if you watch this video. You must do something (watch the video) to gain something (more energy and extra life). That's what programs are: opportunities that can help you get ahead.

The Merriman Online Dictionary defines programs as "a plan or system under which action may be taken toward a goal." The following are a list of programs that may benefit you:

- **Public Housing** is a housing program you probably know well, and of course, they too, have many rules and regulations. If you fit the requirements, you can greatly benefit from paying reduced rent while others pay full price. Public Housing subsidizes rent based on your income. (Search public housing in your area). http://portal.hud.gov/hudportal/HUD?src=/topics/rental_assistance/phprog.

- **The HEAP Program** (Home Energy Assistance Program) may be a part of the weatherization programs in your community. If you have trouble paying your utilities, these programs help those who qualify, and that person just may be you.
  http://www.benefits.gov/benefits/benefit-details/623

- **The Benefits.Gov websites** offer benefits to those in need in their state or local government. SNAP, or the Supplemental Nutrition

Assistance Program (also known as food stamps) is also accessed through Benefits.gov. For further help, see if you have a Benefit Bank in your state (www.thebenefitbank.org). The Benefit Bank online service helps with food assistance, health coverage, home energy assistance and much more." This a GREAT resource. Check it out!

- **The Job Corps** is a free education and training program that helps young people earn a high school diploma or GED and find and keep a good job. For eligible young people at least 16 years of age that qualify as low income, Job Corps provides the all-around skills needed to succeed in a career and life. http://www.jobcorps.gov/Home.aspx

- **The Peace Corps** is an American organization serviced by volunteers sent around the world to promote world peace and cultural understanding. They work at the grassroots level to develop sustainable solutions to address challenges in agriculture, community economic development, education, the environment, health, and youth development. Through their service, volunteers gain a unique cultural understanding and a lifelong commitment to service, positioning them to succeed in today's global economy. To become a volunteer for the Peace Corp, you must be over 18 years old and a U.S. Citizen. http://www.peacecorps.gov

- **AmeriCorps VISTA** members are passionate and committed to their mission to bring individuals and communities out of poverty. Members make a year-long, full-time commitment to serve on a specific project at a nonprofit organization or public agency. They focus on building the administrative and financial capacity of organizations that fight illiteracy, improve health services, foster economic development, and assist low-income communities. A living allowance and medical benefits are provided while working on your mission. To become an AmeriCorps Vista, look into the website below.

(http://www.nationalservice.gov/programs/americorps/americicorps-vista)

These are federal programs that give opportunities for education, jobs and traveling. Some folks take advantage of basic assistance such as food stamps, and subsidized housing, but not as many take advantage of free learning or travel opportunities. Some folks try to push the rules of these programs. Other folks are grateful for the opportunity. Thousands of dollars are available to those who take advantage of these opportunities and even more priceless memories.

Opportunities exist, just look into them!

Outro: Game On!

Whew, that was a lot! And that's just the beginning! This thing called adult life has a lot to offer, but also a lot of things you must know. But it isn't difficult if you learn the rules. Are there exceptions to the rules? Absolutely! But you first must learn the rules to know if you're an exception. Do rules ever get changed or get broken? All the time. But if you are the one breaking the rules, make sure you're ready to deal with the consequences. Can the rules change? Remember, the only thing that will happen in life IS change! You might be the one who'll find an injustice in a rule and change it if it's a better way for others to live and work. That's what life's all about.

There will be ups and downs, triumphs and trials. Not one person on earth, rich or poor, has not had problems in this life. The difference is how one deals with them and moves on. Choose wisely, find trustful people that can help you, and realize that knowing these simple rules will poise you for success. I believe in you! Now get moving!

www.ingramcontent.com/pod-product-compliance
Lightning Source LLC
Chambersburg PA
CBHW071413040426
42444CB00009B/2228